Restaurant Business Secrets:

A Dishwasher's Perspective.

(What Working As A Dishwasher Taught Me About Life)

Kyle Werflow

Table Of Contents:

What this book contains is a short story with a powerful message. I hope you enjoy!

First Straw..
Second Straw...
Third Straw..
Conclusion...

Preface

I was inspired to write this book after obtaining a skill by trade after 6 years of restaurant related experience. Almost immediately after giving my two weeks notice, it dawned on me that I would soon be back in the same position that I found myself at 18 years old when I first entered the workforce.

Re-learning how to FOLLOW instead of lead was out of the norm for me when, for quite some time, I had been a big fish in a small pond. Now inverted, I find myself obligated to share my wealth of knowledge while it is fresh in my mind. For I know that one day I will be able to look back on these experiences and remember what I came from and how I was able to take the reigns in my life at a reasonably young age.

We have no modern day trials for the boy becoming a man. No true role models that teach us how to grab life by the balls. How to mould and forge our own path when it is too easy to conform to societies standards. In my moment of inspiration, I deeply hope to inspire what lies inside of you, the reader. That my tiny impact of you opening this book and feeling these pages allow you to express the amazing spiritual being you are meant to be.

- Courage and Strength

Introduction

Many people think that 'Business' simply has to do with the amount of numbers coming into your bank account, how much of something you are selling, the specific service you provide OR the entertainment you perform.

Very rarely do we ever stop to consider the characteristics that come along with these ventures, and how it moulds the individual into the person that we see before us in our daily lives. Whether looking across from them or the reflection we see in the mirror.

This story is geared toward helping the reader discover within themselves the true power they possess and to merely suggest to them the amount of strength hidden deep within their own reservoirs of free will.

The First Straw

Back when I first turned 18, I thought to myself... shit now that I'm an adult I've got to do adult things. So first thing I did was to stop smoking weed to pass a drug test and then to find a job. Fast forward 30 days and I'm clean so I call the local hall that routinely hosts parties, graduations, weddings, etc, and asked for a job. Almost immediately I was called in for an interview and the goal was accomplished. Woohoo! I thought to myself now im doing adult shit finally and I can go back to smoking weed!!!

Now before I go any further, I am absolutely no stranger to hard work but I had no idea what I was getting myself into. You are probably thinking to yourself - washing dishes isn't hard. Well let me explain. The title "Dishwasher" is a very loosely used term in the food service industry but I didn't know that at the time. It stretches to involve "miscellanious" tasks or things that are minor that have to rarely, but consistently get addressed. Now my family has a farm that I worked on during my summers but things were about to be taken to another level. I can operate with a lot of shit going wrong, but I can only give so many 'straws' if you will. Once they're gone, I'm out of patience.

The first day I show up and the doors are locked. I was confused so i just stood there knocking, and knocking over and over. Finally two dudes came up to the door, ignored me, and started moving the carpet. I gave them the "what the fuck you gonna just look at me?" stare and they let me in. They asked what I was there for and immediately after I told them I was the new guy they turned to each other and grinned. I was very uneasy from this point moving forward. They took me 'under their wing' and told me we had to rearrange chairs in the party room. No big deal, right? I turn down the hallway and I see endless chairs just scattered throughout the dancefloor in stacks of 5 chairs each. Immediately i knew it would be a long day.

After about 2 hours of 'orientation' into this job I said to myself "I thought I was going to work in a kitchen, this isn't what I applied for. I'm not supposed to be a janitor or a mover. The position I applied for was dishwasher and no dishes?" Shortly after we began the real job. This is where things got interesting...

So this guy, lets call him Jerry. Now Jerry was the head dishwasher and had been there for 5 years at this point. He goes onto tell me about the hierarchy, what's expected of me, what's my role, that I don't actually get a 'break' and to not wear anything I actually cared about ruining. Except he kept going on... like a laundry list. When he finished verbally telling me what to do he picked up a pile of string and showed me physically ANOTHER long list of things we had to do. I asked him, aren't we dishwashers? Why do we have to do so much? Isn't there a building manager, janitor, or something like that?

He looks at me dead in the eyes and replied with: "Why do you think you got the job? All these kids quit because being a dishwasher is the most important role in a restuarant business and requires you to put in the most effort of everyone, even the cooks." " Most of the time you'll be doing the waitstaff and the cooks work combined. He went on. "So Imagine a restaurant, or any business for that matter, being a human being. Without the spine, or backbone, the entire being would collapse in a matter of moments and be rendered useless to themselves as well as the rest of society. Hopeless and desperate it would stay there waiting to be rescued as so many businesses are today. However, with the spine the human is able go about it's normal routine without worry or care. That's how you have to think about your role. You are vital to the success of this business. Without you, we fail."

Talk about pressure... I felt I was just crushed with a ton of bricks. Here I am trying to be an adult and do the right thing by getting a job and having my own money. Little did I know by picking the 'least skilled and inexperienced position" I actually got the most work and responsibilty! Who would have thought! Now I'm tired, angry, overwhelmed, and flooded with anxiety. However I hid it well and we moved on.

The first thing Jerry had me do was cut up the salad. Quick, easy, painless. Next I had to cut strawberries and oranges. This is where I realized that restaurants ain't shit, and at the end of the day everything is about reducing waste to increase profits. Unfortunately even sometimes at the expense of the health of the people served. They were all mouldy and smelly. Upon my expression he replied with

"What are you talking about everything here is fresh". I did my job to the best of my ability and moved on. We started with food prep, cleaned the tables then swept and mopped the floor. Right after we finished mopping the floor, and everything was clean this is where things got worse.

The drain to the sink next to the prep tables are not actually attached. The water falls about 2-3 inches into the drain below. Well they were working on the sewers that evening and the pipes began to backup. Within seconds there was human shit and toilet paper pouring out like a geyser. Jerry said, " Quick get the salad bin!" I gave Jerry the bin and he put the salad bin, what we use to prepare and toss the salad ready to be consumed by customers, to now catch shit and toilet paper pouring out. Thank GOD this was brief. The geyser flowed for 15-20 seconds but it was enough that we had to completely mop and throw out several mop heads. My shoes were also fucked for the remainder of the evening. Although the waste was gone, the smell remained. As for the salad bin, I hear rumors it's still used to this day... This was the first straw

The Second Straw

Next up was garbage and recycling. We load up the handtrucks to take out the trash and upon arrival at the dumpster about 50 ft away, we walk into a second sight I could never forget. When we looked into the dumpster before throwing in the trash I witnessed hundreds upon hundreds of rats feasting on all the scraps in this kind of swarm, like honeybees on a honeycomb. We threw the trash in right on top of them and they scattered like a stampede. Immediately they ran towards the building and jumped into a drain coming out the side! I thought what the fuck is going on here. Jerry turned to me and says, "This shit happens all the time no big deal."

We proceeded to clean garbage cans, scrub the walls(yes you read that correctly), scrape and scrub the floors. Help the bartender (ice, glasses, fruits, etc) Then we help the waitstaff (napkins, table cloths, silverware, etc) and then finally we get back to our work station to find it piled high with dishes. My first thought was, "Wow we just helped everyone do their job and they're not going to help us." This was the second straw and at this point I got this feeling of helplessness. This was when I realized what it took to be an adult. And now, this is what I as an adult have to face.

Next comes dinner. It's a banquet type of dinner so all the meals go out at once, and all the roles of the establishment (even the boss) come to stand around the table to plate the food before it's sent out to the customers. The point is to keep everything hot and bang out the orders in about 10-15 minutes. I'm not sure if my boss was drunk or just plain goofy (later on I would find out it's the latter) and would call an order, then get 'confused' go back on it, send out the wrong order, give the wrong table, stop, go, wait, I'll be right back and then leave us for a few moments while the food got cold. Absolutely no order at all in this kitchen. This wasted about an hour and when it was over and I got back to my work station - yep, you guessed it. Another massive pile of dishes and silverware waiting to be cleaned.

I just about finished this load when Jerry comes in and says I have to clean the parking lot. I still had a decent amount of dishes and I wasn't even able to stop to eat dinner but I said Ok. Now remember when I got this job I just wanted some cash and a job because adults get jobs. Now I'm the go to man for every single thing going wrong in this place. I'm 18! I thought to myself, "If this is what being an adult is like, it fucking sucks."

The parking lot was full of glasses, smashed bottles, blunt wrappers, streamers, confetti, clothing, hangers, cans and oh vomit. Lots and lots of vomit. I thought it couldn't get worse until Jerry came out to give me the broom and dust pan to let me know it was for the vomit. Yes, I was expected to clean up vomit that is outside, and could easily be washed away or ignored. This was the second straw.

The Third Straw

Fast forward the party ends and we begin clean up. However in between dinner and midnight it was snowing heavily. The guests were leaving and there was a lot of snow on the ground. So since I was the new guy I had to go outside, and clean off everyone's windshield and dig out their car to the best of my ability. After the last guest departed and I looked up for a sigh of relief, my boss came out and said, " Can you hurry up and do the dishes so I can go home?" It's 1:30 a.m. at this point and I came in at 12 p.m yesterday. This was the third straw. I finished my work and was dismissed.

Now you would think after an experience like this I would say, " fuck that place It's a shithole, I'm never going back, that place should be shut down, how do they run like that, they should be ashamed, They overwork and underpay their employees." And on and on. However, nothing happened. I took it on the chin and continued to work there for the next 6 years until I secured a better job while going to college for a degree I would never use.

That short story is how every weekend would go. So much was being put on me and I just got there. Much later on I found out that they actually tried to make me quit by putting me through all these trials. When I didn't quit and they saw I wasn't leaving anytime soon they actually complemented me and made me the new head Dishwasher. This was the first time I was put in a position to be a leader.

Now why didn't I just quit after the first day? It was basically hell. This would be my weekend life for the next 6 years while I went to school during the week. School to work and right back. Now firstly I was getting plenty of social/ intimate interaction during the weekday so I wasn't missing out on life and being young. I was having my fair share of fun. Second thing is going through such a difficult and frustrating challenge, my first night, was so rewarding when I look back on how it was up to me to keep this boat afloat. Thirdly: Being forced into a position, sometimes, is the best thing that can happen to you. You never know how strong you really are until you have to be. You quite literally must try to put yourself in a position often of sinking or swimming. Hitting or missing. Just going for it, because you may just surprise yourself. Even till this day I am greatful for the experience as hard as it was.

If it wasn't for this experience I might not be the person I am today and know exactly what I want. I also know what I don't want. Sometimes the challenges that are the hardest to make it through have the biggest lessons to be learned. However I wasn't thinking about the lessons I learned scrubbing shit out of my shoes because the pipes under the sink backed up and flooded my shoes with human waste. No, not in the slightest.

Far too often many people think woe is me as something bad is happening to them. Often it takes time to look in hindsight at the message of those experience you have in your life. What this taught me is that though the hardest worker doesn't make the most money he seems to have an awful lot of responsibility. Although he is easily replaceable, he is always needed. There will always be a demand for a dishwasher because since washing dishes is a simple singular act that doesnt take a lot of time, additional resposibilities must be bestowed upon the worker so he doesn't become 'idle'. Through this "pressure" if you will, they will either crumble and quit or succeed and be made into a diamond.

Thank you for reading this short excerpt from my life. As most entry level jobs I expected to make my exit early but something about having to assume responsibility and being forced to lead others brought out a side of me I never could imagine that I possessed. That is how I learned to become a great leader. That is the Restaurant Business Secret that I learned so many years ago which I am confident in relaying to the reader. Without trails you will never become a man. You will stay a boy. Men are leaders. Throw yourself into the metaphorical 'fire' in any field or occupation and test yourself to be the man or woman you know you can be. Show up - because that's 80% of the battle right there. Once you have arrive you'll see that the resistance you were feeling before you left home isn't so strong once you're actually there. It's not because things are difficult that we dare not venture, it's because we dare not venture that things are difficult.

As I write this many years later, I am reliving all of the emotions both positive and negative that have helped mould me into the calm and patient man I am today. Haha even patient enough to write a book! All I ask from the reader is to not wait to reflect on the tough experiences of your life and to see the lessons they present in the now. Often what seems like tough times are simply opportunities to grow and develop yourself more as a person to be able to handle the further struggles of life down the road. These help to develop your character. Even when you lose, you learn. So take every loss as a lesson because life is all about expression and experiences. When living in the now you can view things as they are, and choose who to be at every given moment.

As Bruce Lee once said " Don't pray for an easy life, pray for the strength to endure a difficult one." Welcome Challenges for they are your obstacle. However, welcome rewards for they are your due.

Conclusion

Thank you for reading this book! It would mean a lot to me if you would leave a review if you gained ANY value from this book! It helps authors like myself to gain more exposure and potentially reach even more people to help them see the lessons in their own daily life!

Bonus

If you've purchased the paperback version, you have recieved this bonus for directly supporting me.

This isn't going to be long or exhaustive, but I'd like to share a secret with you.

The secret to living is giving of yourself, your talents, and your gifts to the world.

The second secret is gratitude. For when you combine gratitude and contribution(giving) you find yourself at peace and simultaneously fulfilling all your human needs.

www.ingramcontent.com/pod-product-compliance
Lightning Source LLC
Chambersburg PA
CBHW072240230526
45466CB00025B/2241